Dear Lizzie,
Happy 7th Birthday
Love from,
Leo x x x

Fantastic Footballers

40 inspiring icons

lizzie

Jean-Michel Billioud & Almasty

WIDE EYED EDITIONS

Mad About the Beautiful Game

Who are the **40 greatest players in history?** It's a difficult question to answer because there are so many criteria involved in selecting the best players.

For example, you could base the selection just on technical skills, or on players who have scored the most goals – or who have conceded the least. You could also choose players who have won individual awards or those who have won titles with their club or national team. There's no perfect selection method... apart from the one in this book of course!

Over the pages in this book, you can find out about legendary players such as Pelé, the King of Football, and attacking midfielder Zinédine Zidane. Their studs have left an indelible mark on the beautiful game. But you can also read about today's stars, like Lionel Messi and Cristiano Ronaldo, as well as rising talents such as Paul Pogba and Neymar. It's also very important to include the top female players. For over a century, women's teams and star players like Mia Hamm, Marta and Nadine Angerer have been part of the football world, but they have only recently been properly recognised.

The players in this book create an amazing line-up. It would be almost impossible for a coach to choose the 11 best players from this impressive selection. Some very talented players would be left on the bench!

Contents

21
DIDIER DROGBA

22
GIANLUIGI
BUFFON

23
LUKA MODRIĆ

24
SAMUEL ETO'O

25
ZLATAN
IBRAHIMOVIC

26
MEGAN RAPINOE

27
RONALDO

28
ANDRÉS INIESTA

29
CRISTIANO
RONALDO

30
MOHAMED
SALAH

31
SERGIO RAMOS

32
LIONEL MESSI

33
N'GOLO
KANTÉ

34
PAUL POGBA

35
NEYMAR

36
KYLIAN
MBAPPÉ

37
MIA HAMM

38
ADA HEGERBERG

39
MARTA

40
AMANDINE
HENRY

Alfredo Di Stéfano

WHAT NEXT

Alfredo Di Stéfano went on to coach at a series of top clubs, including Boca Juniors, Valencia CF, River Plate and Real Madrid.

The biggest star at the triumphant Real Madrid of the 1950s, King Pelé himself considers Alfredo Di Stéfano to be the greatest footballer of all time. A charismatic leader, he was a playmaker as well as a prolific centre forward who was the Spanish league's top scorer in five separate seasons. He always chose to use his amazing skills to help his teammates rather than show off. Under the guidance of their maestro, The Whites – Real Madrid's nickname – reigned supreme over European football and become the best club in the world.

AWARDS

Di Stefano won the Ballon d'Or twice, in 1957 and 1959.

Di Stéfano scored **308** goals for Real

MAJOR HONOURS

Copa America (1947)

Argentinian Championship (1945, 1947)

Colombian Championship (1949, 1951, 1952)

La Liga (1954, 1955, 1957, 1958, 1961, 1962, 1963, 1964)

European Cup (1956, 1957, 1958, 1959, 1960)

THE KILLER COMPLIMENT

"I don't know if I was a better player than Pelé, but Di Stéfano was definitely better than him." Diégo Maradona.

THE HIGHPOINT

In 1960, Di Stefano scored a hat-trick (three goals) for his beloved Real Madrid as they thumped German side Eintracht Frankfurt in the European Cup final.

THE PASSING OF TIME

Over the years, his nickname changed from the Blond Arrow to the Divine Bald One.

ONLY REGRET

A torn groin muscle stopped him playing in the 1962 World Cup. He never took part in the biggest event in the football world.

QUICKSILVER

Di Stéfano was the master of the dribble and the short pass.

ARGENTINIAN THEN SPANISH
6 international games and 6 international goals for Argentina 31 international games and 23 goals for Spain

DATES
Born in 1926
Died in 2014

POSITION
Forward

MAIN CLUB
Real Madrid

Undisputed leader

Stanley Matthews

Perhaps the most exciting English attacker of all time, Stanley Matthews tormented defences for almost 30 years. "The Wizard of Dribble" signed his first professional contract at just 17 years old and went on to rack up 698 league appearances for Stoke and Blackpool - eventually retiring at 50! His trickery and skill was beyond compare, with Franz Beckenbauer claiming he was so fast "almost no one in the game could stop him." A selfless team-player, Matthews was known as the master of the assist, laying on countess goals for his teammates throughout his stunning career.

HOBBY

His career was so long because he dedicated his life to keeping fit. He started exercising when he was six, inspired by his father, a professional boxer known as "The Fighting Barber".

29

games played for the England wartime team between 1939 and 1946

MAJOR HONOURS

FA Cup (1953)

Ballon d'Or (1956)

English Second Division (1933, 1963)

THE MATTHEWS FINAL

Matthews' best-ever display came in the 1953 FA Cup final, which will forever be known as "The Matthews Final". He dragged Blackpool from 3-1 down to win 4-3 against Bolton, setting up the winner with a trademark cross.

NOT IN IT FOR THE MONEY

Before signing for Stoke as a player, Matthews worked in the offices at the club. When he eventually put pen to paper on a playing contract, he was paid just £5 a week!

AWARD

Matthews was the first-ever winner of the Ballon d'Or!

ENGLISH
54 international games
11 international goals

DATES
Born in 1915
Died 2000

POSITION
Attacker

MAIN CLUBS
Blackpool, Stoke, Madrid

COOL HEADED
Despite making appearances in more than 700 league games, Matthews was never booked!

DIET
On Thursdays, the only thing Matthews would eat was carrot juice.

DELICATE TOUCH
Even though he was one of the most technically-gifted players in the world, Mathews rarely used his left foot and almost never tackled.

Wing wizard

Ferenc Puskás

WHAT NEXT

As a coach he took unfashionable Greek side Panathinaikos to their first-ever European Cup final in 1971, where they lost 2-0 to Dutch giants Ajax at Wembley.

A key tactician for the Hungarian national team, who lost only one match between 1950 and 1956 – the World Cup final! – Ferenc Puskás was also a star player at Real Madrid at a time when they dominated European football. He formed a formidable double-act with Alfredo Di Stéfano, the pair of them a constant goal-scoring threat. In 1960, Real won the European Cup against Eintracht Frankfurt with three goals from Di Stéfano and four from Puskás.

242
goals in 262 official matches with Real

PLAYER AND SOLDIER

At the start of his career, Puskás was the key player at Budapest Honvéd, the Hungarian Army's official club. This was when he acquired his nickname, the Galloping Major, in reference to the rank he was given.

DOUBLE VICTORY

On 25 November 1953, Hungary became the first team from continental Europe to beat England at home, with a historic match at Wembley Stadium. The Mighty Magyars won 6-3, with two goals from Puskás. Six months later, the English suffered a humiliating defeat in Budapest, losing 7-1.

AWARD

Puskás won the gold medal at the Helsinki Olympic Games.

WORLD CITIZEN

As well as playing for his native Hungary, Puskas also turned out for Spain.

HUNGARIAN THEN SPANISH
85 international games and 84 international goals for Hungary
4 international games for Spain

DATES
Born in 1927
Died in 2006

POSITION
Forward

MAIN CLUBS
Budapest Honvéd, Real Madrid

UNLUCKY

Playing with an ankle inury, Puskás lost the 1954 World Cup final against West Germany.

FORMIDABLE

Puskás had a dangerously accurate and ultra-powerful left foot.

The galloping major

Lev Yashin

Unbeatable in the air, the goalkeeper for the flamboyant Soviet team of the 1960s became a shot-stopping icon. He was the pioneer of modern football, rushing out of his area to block attacks and immediately passing back to his teammates to destabilise his opponents. His charisma, height and exuberance made him an imposing keeper, who saved more than 100 penalties in his career. Strong, fearless and incredibly fast to react, he didn't think twice about throwing himself at the feet of the attackers. He lay down his gloves at the impressive age of 40!

AMAZING SAVE

At the 1960 European Championship final, Yashin pulled off an outstanding feat by saving a free kick from Yugoslav player Bora Kostic, ensuring victory for the Soviet Union.

AWARD

He is the only goalkeeper to have won the Ballon d'Or (in 1963).

MAJOR HONOURS

Olympic gold medal (1956)

European Championship (1960)

Russian (USSR) Championship (1954, 1955, 1957, 1959, 1963)

Russian Cup (1953, 1967, 1970)

ALL-ROUNDER

When he first began to play with Dynamo Moscow, while working as a tool and die maker at the same steelworks as his parents, he also served as the goalkeeper for the Dynamo ice hockey team!

AN ORIGINAL VIEWPOINT

Yashin explained why he came out of his goal so often: "Waiting passively on the white line is easy, simplistic and sometimes even ridiculous. Why deprive the team of an extra player on the pitch when possible?"

812
official matches

THE GOLDEN ERA

Lev Yashin
liked to play
wearing a cap.

ULTRA-FAST

He often threw
the ball like a handball player
to get it back into play quicker.

MAN IN BLACK

His habit of always
dressing in black earned
him the nickname
The Black Spider.

**RUSSIAN
(USSR)**
78 international
games

DATES
Born in 1929
Died in 1990

POSITION
Goalkeeper

CLUB
Dynamo Moscow

Revolutionary goalkeeper

Bobby Charlton

A gentleman on and off the field, Bobby Charlton is one of the greatest players England has ever produced. After emerging as one the "Busby babes" – a crop of exciting young players at Manchester United in the 1950s – Charlton helped the club become kings of the English and European game. He was also England's brightest star as they lifted the World Cup in 1966 in Wembley Stadium, his two goals in the semi-final helping them to the final where they would beat bitter rivals West Germany.

AWARD

Charlton inspired Manchester United to their first ever European Cup in 1968. He hit two goals in a 4-1 extra-time win over Portuguese giants Benfica – led by the legendary Eusebio.

MAJOR HONOURS

English Championship (1957, 1965, 1967)

FA Cup (1963)

European Cup (1968)

World Cup (1966)

World Cup Golden ball (1966)

Ballon d'Or (1966)

TRAGEDY

In 1958, a plane due to take the Manchester United team home from Munich crashed during take off. Charlton was one of 21 survivors, but 23 people were killed, including eight of his team-mates. He dedicated each of his subsequent triumphs to them.

KING OF THE WORLD

Charlton booked England's place in the World Cup final in 1966 with both goals against Portugal in a 2-1 semi-final win – first slotting home from a rebounded effort and then smashing into the bottom corner from the edge of the box.

49

goals for England: a record until broken by Wayne Rooney until 2015

ENGLISH
106 international games
49 international goals

DATES
Born in 1937

POSITION
Attacking midfielder

MAIN CLUB
Manchester United

HAIR WE GO

Charlton was famous for his signature comb-over hairstyle.

GREAT GOALS

Charlton scored 249 goals for Manchester United: a record until it was broken in 2016. By who? You guessed it.... Wayne Rooney!

TWO-FOOTED

Charlton was able to hit the ball with great power using either foot.

The true gent

Garrincha

Despite his amazing skills, Vasco de Gama, Fluminense, and Flamengo all refused to sign up the young Garrincha.

1

defeat in 50 national games

An exceptionally gifted attacker, Manoel Francisco dos Santos, known by his nickname Garrincha (little bird), was an unpredictable and unstoppable force on the pitch. He was an idol in his native Brazil in the 1950s and 1960s. His famous weaving dribble meant that he almost always got the better of the defenders, with a feint to the left then a sudden turn to the right with the outside of his foot – a simple movement executed at breakneck speed. Sadly, Garrincha became an alcoholic, eventually fell into poverty and died aged 49.

PHILOSOPHY

He was inspiring both on and off the pitch, winning over journalists and supporters with his common sense: "Winning the World Cup? It's really very easy, because there are only six games, and no return matches either!"

FAIR PLAY

In the semi-final of the 1962 World Cup, Garrincha was sent off for kicking a Chilean player on the bottom. But he still got to play in the final... and win it!

GLAMOUR

Garrincha and the singer Elza Soarés made a glamorous couple who were hugely popular in Brazil. The press and their fans followed every little thing the queen of samba and prince of football said and did – their arguments as well as their extravagant parties.

MAJOR HONOURS

World Cup (1958, 1962)

Champion of the state of Rio de Janeiro (1957, 1961, 1962)

Joint top scorer at the World Cup (1962)

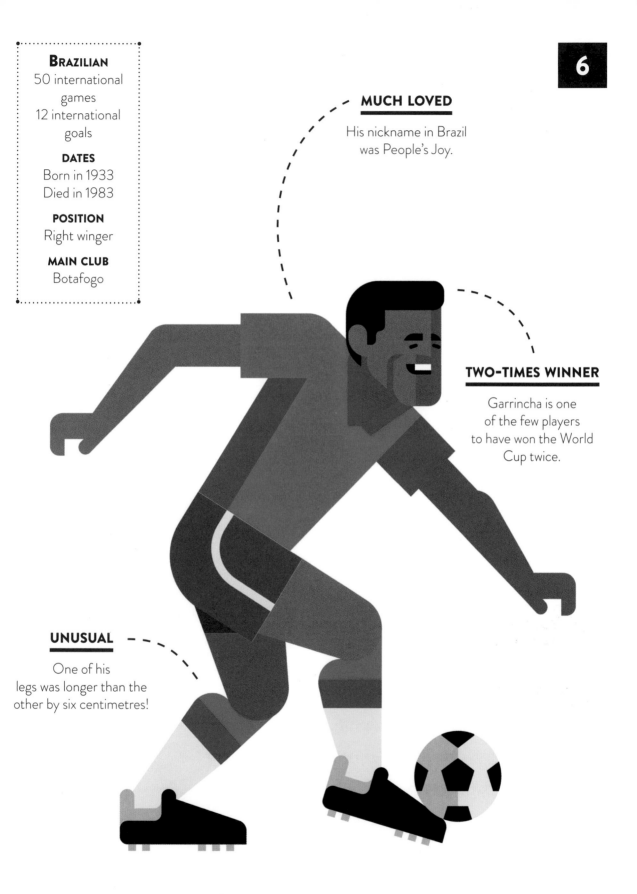

BRAZILIAN
50 international games
12 international goals

DATES
Born in 1933
Died in 1983

POSITION
Right winger

MAIN CLUB
Botafogo

MUCH LOVED
His nickname in Brazil was People's Joy.

TWO-TIMES WINNER
Garrincha is one of the few players to have won the World Cup twice.

UNUSUAL
One of his legs was longer than the other by six centimetres!

Free as a bird

Pelé

A PRECOCIOUS GENUIS

Pelé is the youngest player and youngest goal-scorer to win the football World Cup. In the years since his celebrated achievements, there have been a few younger players in the competition – but they haven't managed to win it.

LEGENDARY GOAL

During a match between Fluminense and his club Santos on 5 March 1961, Pelé got past seven players and scored one of the most spectacular goals of his career in front of 120,000 people.

Arguably the world's greatest ever player, Edson Arantes do Nascimento – known more commonly as Pele – won his first World Cup aged just 17, and went on to leave a lasting mark on the World Cup and football history. Brazil is famed as a breeding ground for footballing talent, but Pelé will always remain king. Gifted with raw natural talent, electrifying pace and the ability to create incredible moves on the pitch, the legendary number 10 thrilled stadiums the world over and went on to win two more World Cups.

MAJOR HONOURS

World Cup
(1958, 1962, 1970)

Copa Libertadores
(1962, 1963)

Intercontinental Cup
(1962, 1963)

Brazilian Championship
(1961, 1962, 1963, 1964, 1965, 1968)

American Championship
(1977)

WHAT NEXT

Pelé starred in lots of advertisements and later went into politics, serving as the Minister for Sport in Brazil between 1995 and 1998, with a focus on reducing corruption in Brazilian football.

GOLDEN BOY

After Brazil's victory in the 1958 World Cup final in Sweden – thanks in no small part to the two goals that he scored – a delighted Pelé collapsed in the arms of his teammate Didi, who was almost 12 years older than him!

77
goals scored for Brazil

BRAZILIAN
92 international games
77 international goals

DATES
Born in 1940

POSITION
Forward

MAIN CLUBS
Santos FC, New York Cosmos

WINNER

Pelé is the only player in history to have won three World Cups.

BORN STRIKER!

The prolific Pelé scored more than 1,000 goals in his career. Although the official number is disputed, some football historians believe he netted as many as 1,284.

FAVOURITE TARGET

During the 1966 World Cup, the unstoppable Pelé was constantly fouled by defenders.

The king of forwards

Bobby Moore

WHAT NEXT

After winning the World Cup, Moore became a huge celebrity and did lots of modelling work.

The best defender the world had ever seen, according to Pele, Bobby Moore remains the undisputed hero of English football, having captained his country to its first and only World Cup triumph in 1966. He was way ahead of his time as a player, combining tough-tackling with exquisite passing ability – qualities seen in very few defenders of his era. He was also a legend at West Ham, the club he captained for most of his career. With Moore at the centre of everything, they won the FA Cup for the first time ever and the Cup Winners' Cup.

FAIR PLAY

Moore was seen as one of the fairest defenders the game has ever seen, embodying the Corinthian spirit of honest endeavour.

MAJOR HONOURS

FA Cup (1964)

Cup Winners' Cup (1965)

World Cup (1966)

TOO SOON

Moore was diagnosed with cancer in 1964, just two years before the historic World Cup win. Despite recovering, the illness returned in 1991 and he passed away two years later at the age of 51.

RESPECT

A picture of Moore and Pelé swapping shirts after England lost to Brazil in the 1970 World Cup was beamed across the world and embodied everything great about Moore. A gentleman even in defeat, the gesture was a mark of respect between two of football's greats.

6

The number he always wore. In 2008, West Ham retired the No 6 shirt so no other player can ever wear it

ICON

A bronze bust of Moore can be found in the entrance foyer of the stand at West Ham's Boleyn Ground.

ENGLISH
108 international games
2 international goals

DATES
Born in 1941
Died in 1993

POSITION
Central defender

MAIN CLUBS
West Ham, Fulham

PASS MASTER

His passing was unrivalled for a defender. He even set up two goals in the 1966 World Cup final.

TIME KEEPER

He always timed his tackles to perfection. His tackle on Brazil's Jairzinho in 1970 is one of football's most famous.

England's leader

Franz Beckenbauer

TRANSFER
In 1977, he astounded everyone by joining New York Cosmos.

Beckenbauer started his career as a midfielder before switching to sweeper and becoming the best defender in the world in the mid-1970s. *Der Kaiser* reigned supreme over his penalty area, his gift for reading the game and delivering pinpoint passes making him a formidable opponent. As a charismatic captain for both club and country, he led Bayern Munich to the European Cup three seasons running (1974, 1975 and 1976) and skippered the West German national team to World Cup glory in 1974.

MAJOR HONOURS

Cup Winners' Cup (1967)

World Cup (1974)

European Championship (1972)

European Cup (1974, 1975, 1976)

Intercontinental Cup (1976)

German Championship (1969, 1972, 1973, 1974, 1982)

American Championship (1977, 1978, 1980)

He wore the captain's armband

50

times for the West German national team

HIS LEGENDARY MATCH

An image from the semi-final of the 1970 World Cup between West Germany and Italy was seen around the world: the German defender played with a dislocated collarbone in a sling for 50 minutes.

HISTORY REPEATS ITSELF

Beckenbauer won the World Cup as both a player (1974) and a manager (1990). He was also a losing finalist as both – as a player in 1966 and a manager in 1986.

AWARDS
He was awarded two Ballons d'Or (1972 and 1976).

GERMAN
103 international games
14 international goals

DATES
Born in 1945

POSITION
Sweeper

MAIN CLUB
Bayern Munich

CLASSY!

He was nicknamed *Der Kaiser*, meaning emperor, because of his influence on the game as well as his imposing presence.

DIFFERENT OPTIONS

He didn't have a fixed number, alternately wearing 4, 5 and 6 over the years.

UNIQUE

Beckenbauer and Brazil's Mario Zagallo are the only two men to have won the World Cup as both players and managers.

Imperial and confident

George Best

MAJOR HONOURS

European Cup (1968)

Premier League (1965, 1967)

English FA Cup (1963)

Born in a working-class area of Belfast, the right winger left his mark on football without ever playing in the finals of a World Cup or European Championship! As famous for his off-field antics as he was for his incredible talent, Manchester United's number 7 was constantly coming up with new moves on the pitch. In 1968, he led his club to its first European Cup victory and received the Ballon d'Or. He was only 22. Tragically, Best became an alcoholic and suffered financial and health problems before dying at age 59.

INCREDIBLE

The international airport at Belfast is named after George Best.

17

different clubs welcomed him as a player

HIS LEGENDARY MATCH

On 29 May 1968, Wembley Stadium hosted the European Cup final between Manchester United and Benfica. Best scored early on in extra time, opening the way for Manchester United's first ever victory in the competition (4-1).

A MISCHIEVOUS PLAYER

In 1976, before playing against the Netherlands with the Northern Irish national team, George Best announced that he was planning to nutmeg Dutch star Johan Cruyff. After he succeeded, he threw his arms in the air as though he had just scored.

EL BEATLE

One of the first
celebrity footballers,
he was jokingly called
the fifth Beatle.

LADIES' MAN

In 1968,
he received up to
10,000 letters of fan
mail a week.

NORTHERN IRISH
37 international
games
9 international
goals

DATES
Born in 1946
Died in 2005

POSITION
Right winger or
center forward

MAIN CLUB
Manchester
United

TWO GOLDEN FEET

A genius,
two-footed dribbler,
he was the top goal scorer
for Manchester United
in four separate seasons.

Aptly named

Johan Cruyff

403

goals in 713 official matches

The best attacker in Europe in the 1970s, Johan Cruyff remains one of the greatest footballers of all time. An uncontainable striker and playmaker, he won three consecutive European Cups with Ajax Amsterdam. Then, at Barcelona, he continued to dazzle. The 1974 World Cup was the scene of his most stunning feats. Despite the fact that the Netherlands lost the final, Cruyff was the star of the tournament. He went on to become a coach, and continued to create attacking and spectacular football.

HEAD TURNER

The legendary "Cruyff Turn" was named after the Dutchman. Invented by Paraguyan Eulogio Martinez Ramiro, Cruyff perfected the sublime skill of faking to pass or shoot and then dragging the ball back through the legs and turning in the opposite direction.

HIS LEGENDARY GOAL

On 22 December 1973, Johan Cruyff's Barcelona played Atlético Madrid. The Barcelona star leaped on a cross from the left and, in mid-air, deflected the ball into the Madrid goal – with his heel!

SLENDER AND SWIFT

He was known as *El Flaco* (the Skinny One) when he played for Barcelona.

THE ONE AND ONLY

His star status meant that he didn't wear the three Adidas stripes on his sleeves like his teammates in the Dutch national team due to an exclusive advertising contract with another brand.

DUTCH
48 international games
33 international goals

DATES
Born in 1947
Died in 2016

POSITION
Attacker

MAIN CLUBS
Ajax Amsterdam, Barcelona

A SPECIAL NUMBER

Johan Cruyff almost always wore the number 14 shirt.

The flying dutchman

Cha Bum-Kun

AWARD

He was voted Asia's Player of the Century.

The greatest icon of Asian football, this South Korean forward rose to fame in Germany in the late 1970s. He was voted the best foreign player in 1980 and won two European Cups, with Eintracht Frankfurt then Bayer Leverkusen. Dynamic and resourceful, Cha Bum-Kun became a star in Germany at a time when the Bundesliga was the most difficult competition. He played his first international match at 19, taking part, without much success, in the 1986 World Cup in Mexico as a player, then the 1998 World Cup in France as the manager.

TRANSFER

Cha Bum-Kun left South Korea for Germany in order to improve his game. He later returned to South Korea and set up youth clubs to develop the next generation of footballers there.

372

matches in the Bundesliga

SERIAL STRIKER

When he stopped playing in Germany in 1989, Cha Bum-Kun held the record for the number of goals scored by a foreign player in the Bundesliga, notching up an impressive 98 goals.

LIKE FATHER LIKE SON

Cha Bum-Kun's son was also a footballer and, like his father, he played at Eintracht Frankfurt. They are one of twenty or so fathers-and-sons who have both played in a World Cup, including the Djorkaeffs, Forlans and Maldinis.

MAJOR HONOURS

UEFA Cup (1980, 1988)

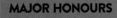

West German Cup (1981)

SOUTH KOREAN
121 international games
55 international goals
DATES
Born in 1953

POSITION
Forward

MAIN CLUBS
Eintracht Frankfurt, Bayer Leverkusen

A POWERFUL LEAP

He scored lots of goals from headers, despite his modest size.

MAKING SPACE

When he ran along the goal line with his long strides, no one could stop him.

GENTLEMAN

Cha Bum-Kun only received one yellow card in his entire career. People said fair play was like a religion for him.

Bum-Bum

Michel *Platini*

DECLARATION

"I died on 17 May 1985." (The day of his final match, aged 32.)

"**See before the others,**" said his father, taking him to training, and Platini took this advice. He loved uncomplicated football, was an outstanding creative player, an exceptional goal-scorer and revitalised French football, which had been in the doldrums. Whether with his national team or Juventus, where he ended his career, he was a leader on and off the pitch. Famed for the accuracy of his free kicks as well as his goal-scoring – exceptional for a midfielder – he won every major competition except the World Cup.

AWARDS

He won three Ballons d'Or (1983, 1984, 1985)

41

goals in 72 appearances for France

MAJOR HONOURS

European Championship (1984)

European Champion Clubs' Cup (1985)

Cup Winners' Cup (1984)

French Championship (1981)

Serie A (1984–1986)

UEFA Super Cup (1984)

UNLUCKY

Michel Platini captained the French team that lost to Germany in the famous 1982 World Cup semi-final. He scored a penalty in the match which finished 3-3 after extra-time and another in the resulting penalty shootout, but they were still eliminated.

LEGENDARY GOALS

In 1978, during a match against Italy, Michel Platini scored a free kick that was unjustly disallowed by the referee. Later in the game, the referee awarded another free kick to France, and Platini scored again!

FRENCH
72 international games
41 international goals

DATES
Born in 1955

POSITION
Attacking midfielder

CLUBS
Nancy, Saint-Étienne, Juventus

THE BOSS!
A leader on the pitch, he was also head of UEFA from 2007 to 2016.

FREE KICK
Platini was a free kick specialist.

10 OUT OF 10
Platini alawys wore the number 10 shirt, whether playing for club or country.

King of the free kick

Diego Maradona

A **star from the very beginning**, the Argentinian midfielder was at the height of his powers during the mid-1980s, a player of boundless natural skill and creativity. Sometimes an angel, sometimes a devil, Diego Maradona won the 1986 World Cup for Argentina and was voted player of the tournament, with five goals, five assists and numerous memorable moments. One of the all-time great dribblers, Maradona also wrote his name in the history books with Napoli, a modest club he led to become champions of Italy and in Europe.

DECLARATION

"My mother thinks I am the best. And I was raised to always believe what my mother tells me."

21
World Cup matches

HITTING THE HEADLINES

Maradona didn't cease to hit the World Cup headlines in 1986... He was sent home from the 1994 tournament after failing a drugs test, but returned to the competition later in his career as a manager and led Argentina to victory at the 2010 World Cup.

THE HAND OF GOD

England met Argentina in the 1986 World Cup in Mexico, four years after the Falklands conflict. Argentina took its revenge on the pitch, with two goals from Maradona: one was a hand ball, the other a work of genius.

MAJOR HONOURS

World Cup (1986)

Argentinian Championship (1981)

Italian Championship (1987, 1990)

UEFA Cup (1989)

ARGENTINIAN
91 international games
34 international goals

DATES
Born in 1960

POSITION
Attacking midfielder

MAIN CLUBS
Argentinos Juniors, Barcelona, Napoli

POCKET SIZE
Just 1.65 metres tall, Maradona is the smallest of football's major stars.

SPECTACULAR
A left-footed wizard, he loved to score from lobs and volleys.

AMAZING TECHNIQUE!
Michel Platini used to say: "What Zidane did with a football, Maradona could do with an orange."

El pibe de oro (The golden kid)

Eusébio

An instant hit at Benfica in Lisbon, Eusébio da Silva Ferreira, known as Eusébio, scored a hat-trick on his debut in 1961. Born in Mozambique, occupied at the time by the Portuguese, he went on to become seven-time top-scorer in the Portuguese championship. The centre forward with a ferocious right foot helped his club to eleven titles, keeping them among the top European clubs for over a decade. He also led Portugal to the semi-finals of the 1966 World Cup, ending the tournament as its leading scorer, with nine goals.

NATIONAL HERO

After he died, tens of thousands of people turned out to watch as his coffin was transferred to the Portuguese national Pantheon. The procession travelled past Benfica's ground, where a statue of the fallen star was erected.

MAJOR HONOURS

European Cup (1962)

Portuguese Championship (1961, 1963, 1964, 1965, 1967, 1968, 1969, 1971, 1972, 1973, 1975)

Portuguese Cup (1962, 1964, 1969, 1970, 1972)

European Cup finalist (1963, 1965, 1968)

PRECOCIOUS TALENT

During the 1962 European Cup final, Eusébio scored two goals in three minutes, helping his club claim the trophy. By the time he was just 20, the young centre forward had already cemented his place as one of the biggest stars of European football.

473

goals in 440 matches with Benfica

TRANSFER

The Portuguese dictator Antonio Salazar refused to sanction the transfer of Eusébio despite interest from a host of Europe's top clubs.

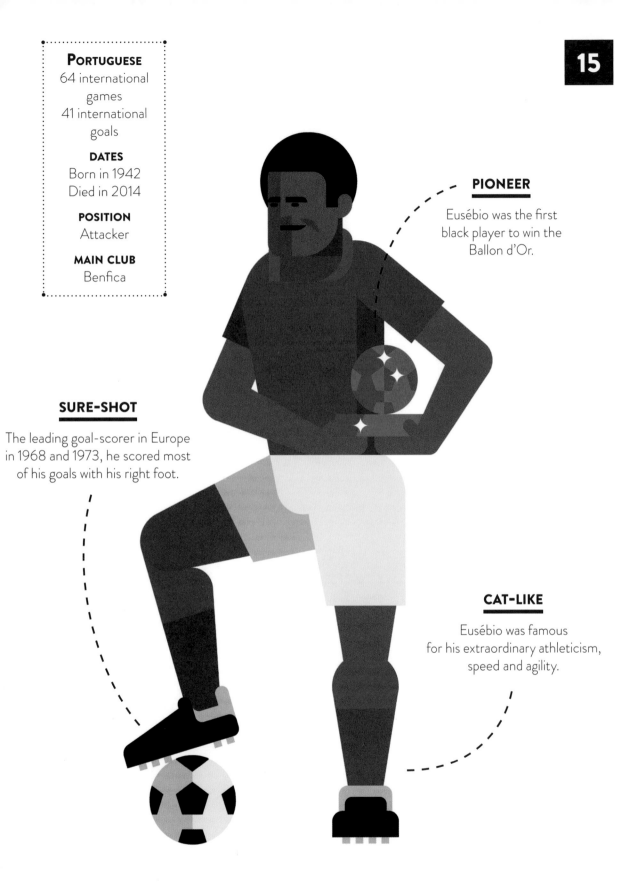

15

PORTUGUESE
64 international games
41 international goals

DATES
Born in 1942
Died in 2014

POSITION
Attacker

MAIN CLUB
Benfica

PIONEER
Eusébio was the first black player to win the Ballon d'Or.

SURE-SHOT
The leading goal-scorer in Europe in 1968 and 1973, he scored most of his goals with his right foot.

CAT-LIKE
Eusébio was famous for his extraordinary athleticism, speed and agility.

The black panther

Marco *van Basten*

WHAT NEXT

Marco van Basten went on to coach the Netherlands before he was 40, from 2004 to 2008. Under his watch the national team qualified for the Euros and the World Cup.

276

goals in 373 professional matches

Tall, powerful, and technically gifted, Dutch centre forward Marco van Basten was four-time top scorer in the Dutch championship, twice top scorer in Serie A, and Europe's leading attacking player at the end of the 1980s. Alongside fellow Dutch stars Ruud Gullit and Frank Rijkaard, Van Basten and co helped AC Milan dominate Italian football in the late 1980s and early 1990s. The trio also inspired the Netherlands to their only ever international trophy, the European Championships in 1988, where the striker was voted the tournament's best player.

MAJOR HONOURS

European Championship (1988)

Cup Winners' Cup (1987)

European Cup (1989, 1990)

European Super Cup (1989, 1990)

Intercontinental Cup (1989, 1990)

Dutch Championship (1982, 1983, 1985)

Serie A (1988, 1992, 1993)

HANDING OVER

Marco van Basten signed his first professional contract with Ajax Amsterdam and played his first match the following year, replacing... Johan Cruyff!

LEGENDARY GOAL

During the Euro 88 finals in Germany, Marco van Basten scored a volleyed goal from an impossibly tight angle. This was the greatest goal in the history of the tournament and he scored it at the age of 23. The match was against the USSR.

AWARDS

Van Basten won the Ballon d'Or three times, in 1988, 1989 and 1992.

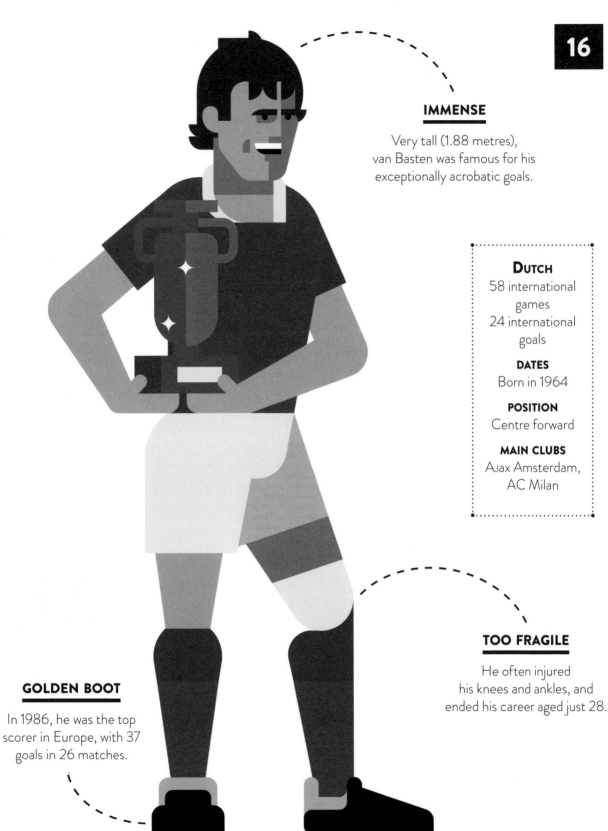

IMMENSE

Very tall (1.88 metres),
van Basten was famous for his
exceptionally acrobatic goals.

DUTCH
58 international
games
24 international
goals

DATES
Born in 1964

POSITION
Centre forward

MAIN CLUBS
Ajax Amsterdam,
AC Milan

TOO FRAGILE

He often injured
his knees and ankles, and
ended his career aged just 28.

GOLDEN BOOT

In 1986, he was the top
scorer in Europe, with 37
goals in 26 matches.

The scoring machine

George Weah

An exceptional goal-scorer, fast and technically gifted, Liberian footballer George Weah enjoyed an extraordinary club career. After one season with Tonnerre de Yaoundé in Cameroon, the powerful forward came to Europe where he played with top-level teams such as Monaco, Paris Saint-Germain, AC Milan, Chelsea and Manchester City. Unfortunately, Weah never had the opportunity to play in a World Cup, but he made Liberia known around the world as he became the first African star to win the Ballon d'Or.

MAJOR HONOURS

Liberian Cup (1986)

Liberian Championship (1987)

Cameroonian Championship (1988)

French Championship (1994)

French Cup (1991, 1993, 1995)

Serie A (1996, 1999)

FA Cup (2000)

A GIFT FROM THE SKIES

Arsène Wenger, his manager at Monaco, described him like this: "Weah was a great surprise. Like the chocolate bunny a kid finds in their garden at Easter. I've never known a player since who's just taken off like that."

A LEGENDARY SLALOM

The prolific goal-scoring Weah scored his most memorable goal for AC Milan, playing against Verona. From a corner taken by the opposition, he controlled the ball in his own penalty area before dribbling the length of the pitch, passing seven defenders and nervelessly beating the keeper.

WHAT NEXT

After hanging up his boots, Weah stood for election as president of Liberia in 2005, but he was not successful. He was elected as a senator in 2014.

PEAK POWERS

The Liberian forward
was a powerful header of the ball.

LIBERIAN
60 international
games
22 international
goals

DATES
Born in 1966

POSITION
Attacker

MAIN CLUBS
Monaco, PSG,
AC Milan

SUPERSTITIOUS

For important matches,
George Weah liked to wear
red boots.

WHAT AN ATHLETE !

His long legs and powerful
physique helped him beat
defenders time and time again.

Mister George

Paolo Maldini

At the age of just 16, Paolo Maldini played his first match for AC Milan. It was a club he would never leave. Alongside his teammates, Franco Baresi, Alessandro Costacurta and Mauro Tassotti, he formed part of a steely defense that went unbeaten for 58 consecutive matches. Maldini had three gifts not often seen in a defender: he was an excellent dribbler who could deliver accurate crosses on the counterattack, and a was model of fair play! He had less success in national colours, losing with Italy in the finals of the 1994 World Cup and at Euro 2000.

902

matches with AC Milan, his one and only club

AWARDS

Paolo Maldini won the European Cup 5 times.

MAJOR HONOURS

World Cup finalist (1994)

Champions League (1989, 1990, 1994, 2003, 2007)

Intercontinental Cup (1989, 1990)

Serie A (1988, 1992, 1993, 1994, 1996, 1999, 2004)

Italian Cup (2003)

UEFA Super Cup (1989, 1990, 1994, 2003)

A FAMILY AFFAIR

In 2003, Paolo Maldini won the Champions League, mirroring his father Cesare who won it in 1963. This is a feat that has only happened twice in the history of football, with the Busquets family at Barcelona and the Sanchis family at Real Madrid.

INDESTRUCTIBLE

Paolo Maldini played in four World Cup tournaments from 1990 to 2002, appearing in a total of 23 matches! Only the German Lotthar Matthaus has played in more (25). But unlike Matthaus, Maldini was never a World Cup winner.

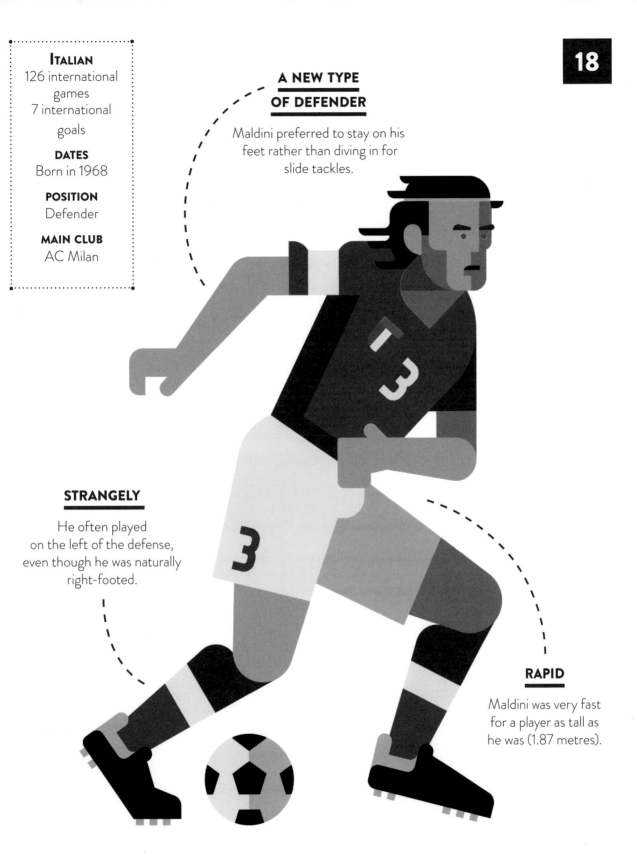

ITALIAN
126 international
games
7 international
goals

DATES
Born in 1968

POSITION
Defender

MAIN CLUB
AC Milan

A NEW TYPE OF DEFENDER

Maldini preferred to stay on his feet rather than diving in for slide tackles.

STRANGELY

He often played on the left of the defense, even though he was naturally right-footed.

RAPID

Maldini was very fast for a player as tall as he was (1.87 metres).

Italian class

Zinédine Zidane

MAJOR HONOURS

World Cup
(1998)

European
Championship
(2000)

Intercontinental
Cup (1996, 2002)

Serie A
(1997, 1998)

La Liga
(2003)

Champions League
(2002)

UEFA Super Cup
(1996, 2002)

AWARD

He won the Champions League in 2016, his first year as manager of Real Madrid.

108

international games for France

A player with jaw-dropping dribbling skills, prince of the step-over and drag-back, Zinédine Zidane was a player with extravagant technical gifts. His vision of the game and anticipation made him one of the all-time great attacking midfielders. His talents were rewarded with the Ballon d'Or in 1998 and the Golden Ball at the World Cup in 2006. He retired from playing the same year, moving swiftly into coaching so that he could stay in football.

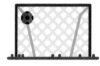

HOT-HEADED

He was shown 14 red cards in his 18-year career. In what would be his final act as a player, the Frenchman head-butted Italian Marco Materazzi in the 2006 World Cup final, which Italy would go on to win after a penalty shootout.

HIS LEGENDARY MATCH

The quarter-final of the 2006 World Cup against Brazil is remembered as Zidane's greatest match. "I count myself lucky to have seen [...] one of the greatest ever solo performances," wrote the Brazilian journalist Juca Kfouri.

GOALS

He scored three times in a World Cup final, two goals in 1998 and one in 2006.

HEADSTRONG

He scored
two headers in the final
of the 1998 World Cup,
as France beat
Brazil 3-0.

FRENCH
108 international
games
31 international
goals

DATES
Born in 1972

POSITION
Attacking
midfielder

MAIN CLUBS
Bordeaux,
Juventus,
Real Madrid

FAVOURITE NUMBER

Number 10 in the French team,
a worthy successor
to Platini.

10

MAGIC FEET

Supremely gifted,
he was a master
of nutmegs, dribbles
and drag-backs.

All the skills

David Beckham

WHAT NEXT

David Beckham has retired from football, but still earns millions every year from advertising. He has made cameo appearances in several films, including *Bend It Like Beckham.*

1st

England player to receive 2 red cards!

A gifted midfielder, David Beckham was the key playmaker at Manchester United in the 1990s, where he won a historic treble in 1999 of the FA Cup, Premier League, and the Champions League, beating Bayern Munich in the final. He then transferred to Real Madrid, where he became one of the galacticos, and was voted the club's player of the year for 2005–2006, winning Spain's La Liga the following season. A shock move to LA Galaxy in 2007 followed, leading to a huge increase in the popularity of football in the US.

MAJOR HONOURS

Champions League (1999)

Premier League (1996, 1997, 1999, 2000, 2001, 2003)

English FA Cup (1999)

Intercontinental Cup (1999)

La Liga (2007)

French Championship (2013)

MLS (2011, 2012)

LEGENDARY GOAL

17 August 1996, David Beckham and Manchester United were playing Wimbledon in the FA Cup. The 20-year-old Beckham scored his first famous goal, a mind-blowing lob from inside his own half!

MAGIC NUMBER

Beckham had the privilege of wearing the legendary number 7 at Manchester United: "It was never my shirt. It was George Best's, Bryan Robson's, Eric Cantona's. The only reason I wanted to wear the number 7 shirt was because of those players."

FAIR PLAY

He was the first England captain to be sent off.

LEADER

David Beckham captained England 59 times.

ENGLISH
115 international games
17 international goals

DATES
Born in 1975

POSITION
All-purpose midfielder

MAIN CLUBS
Manchester United,
Real Madrid,
LA Galaxy,
AC Milan, PSG

METRO MAN

A celebrity model, he was always carefully groomed, even on the pitch.

LIFT OFF

He had one of the most accurate right foots in the world – his long passing was supreme and he was a master of the free-kick.

Footballing icon

Didier Drogba

Didier Drogba was something of a late bloomer. He played in the lower leagues in France before announcing himself at Marseille and later moving to England in 2004 to play for Chelsea. Powerful and quick, he was a fearsome opponent on the ground and in the air, known for his thunderous pinpoint strikes. African Footballer of the year in 2006 and 2009, he also led Chelsea to the Champions League final in 2012. With his side 1-0 down to Bayern Munich, Drogba scored the equaliser before slamming home the decisive penalty in the shootout as Chelsea claimed Europe's top prize for the first time in their history.

AWARD

In 2016, he was voted Chelsea's greatest ever player by the club's supporters.

104

goals in the Premier League

MAJOR HONOURS

Champions League (2012)

Premier League (2005, 2006, 2010, 2015)

League Cup (2005, 2007, 2012)

FA Cup (2007, 2009, 2010, 2012)

Turkish Championship (2013)

CHARITABLE

In 2007, Didier Drogba created a foundation to help tackle health and education problems for the people of Côte d'Ivoire and the rest of Africa. He opened his first clinic in 2014.

AN ICON

In 2006, Côte d'Ivoire qualified for the World Cup for the first time, and team captain Didier Drogba scored the team's first goal of the finals, against Argentina.

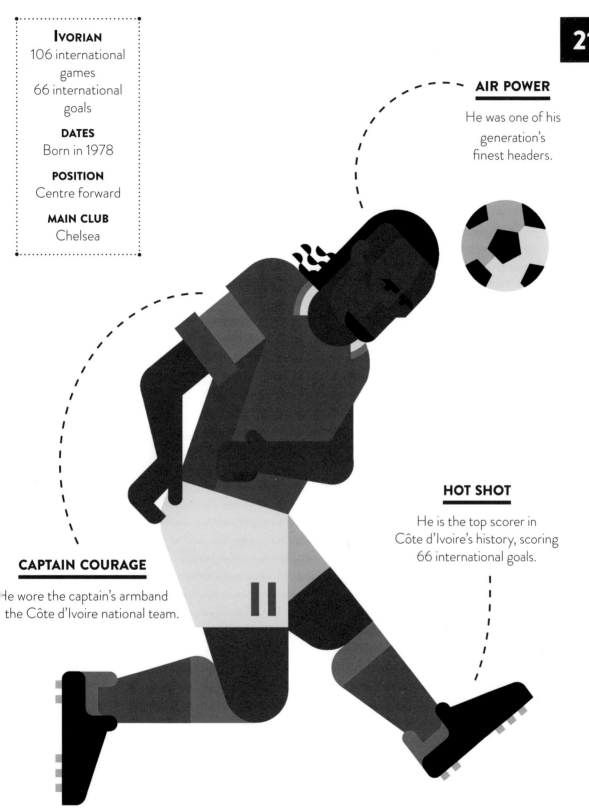

21

IVORIAN
106 international games
66 international goals

DATES
Born in 1978

POSITION
Centre forward

MAIN CLUB
Chelsea

AIR POWER
He was one of his generation's finest headers.

CAPTAIN COURAGE
He wore the captain's armband the Côte d'Ivoire national team.

HOT SHOT
He is the top scorer in Côte d'Ivoire's history, scoring 66 international goals.

Superstar and statesman

Gianluigi Buffon

After first making his name as a **17-year-old with Parma,** the graceful goalkeeper moved to Turin to join Juventus. With a career extending over more than 20 seasons, 700 club games and 150 matches for Italy, Buffon has become a legend and stands as one of football's all-time great goalkeepers: he played in five World Cups, and has one winner's medal! Seemingly ageless, in 2016 at the age of 38 he beat the Italian record for the number of minutes without conceding, going unbeaten in Serie A for 973 minutes, the equivalent of over ten matches.

AMAZING SAVE

In the final of the 2006 World Cup against France, Buffon kept out a powerful Zidane header that everybody thought was a certain goal.

INCREDIBLE

He chose to be a goalkeeper at the age of 12, inspired by Thomas Nkono, the Cameroon goalkeeper who performed heroically during the 1990 World Cup in Italy.

164

international games for Italy

PRICELESS

Juventus broke their transfer record to sign him from Parma: the £33-million fee made him the world's most expensive goalkeeper at the time.

WORLD CHAMPION!

In the 2006 World Cup final against France, he put in a stunning display, with a string of impressive saves as the game finished 0-0 after 90 minutes. Another awesome stop in extra-time denied France a late victory and the Italians went on to win the final after a penalty shootout.

MAJOR HONOURS

World Cup (2006)

Serie A
(2002, 2003, 2012–2016)

Best goalkeeper in the world (2003, 2004, 2006, 2007)

UEFA Cup (1999)

22

ITALIAN
164 international games
DATES
Born in 1978

POSITION
Goalkeeper

MAIN CLUBS
Parma, Juventus

CAT-LIKE

He can stretch his 1.91-metre frame to reach balls that appear unsaveable!

NATURAL LEADER

Always quick to say what he thinks, whether it's advice, criticism or encouragement!

SUPERMAN

Buffon likes to wear a t-shirt with Superman's logo on under his strip.

Classy Gigi

Luca Modrić

Captain of the Croatian national team that reached the 2018 World Cup final, Luka Modrić can do pretty much anything with a football. A talented player from a young age, he grew up in Croatia, a country that gained its independence in 1991 after the break-up of Yugoslavia. He is just as strong in attack as he is in defence. Modrić won the Croatian championship three times before leaving his home country and playing for Tottenham. But it was when he moved to Real Madrid in 2012 that the "Cruyff of the Balkans" really became a star.

AWARDS

In 2018, he was the first Croatian player to win the Ballon d'Or.

> "I've always thought that if I wanted to reach a certain level, I would only manage it through hard work, sacrifice and struggle."

DIFFICULT CHILDHOOD

When he was six years old, Luka Modrić had to leave his village to escape the fighting that gripped his country. He and his family lived for many years as refugees in a hotel.

3
consecutive Champions League titles

ON TOP OF THE WORLD

In 2018, Luka Modrić reached the final of the World Cup and was chosen as the player of the tournament. To top it all off, he also won the Ballon d'Or.

23

CROATIAN
76 international games

DATES
Born 9th September 1985

POSITION
Midfielder

MAIN CLUBS
Tottenham, Real Madrid

NO GIANT
Although he is a giant of the football world, he is 1.72 metres tall.

LASER VISION
He has exceptional eyesight and spots opportunities seemingly before they are even there.

A BRAVE LEADER
He is the proud captain of the Croation national team.

The midfield metronome

Samuel Eto'o

Cameroonian legend Samuel Eto'o played for eleven different clubs and is one of the select group to have played for Real Madrid as well as Barcelona! Whoever he was playing for, he always had a great eye for goal. He scored 129 goals in 199 matches for Barcelona, and 53 times in 102 matches for Inter Milan. Captain of the Cameroon national team, he led the Indomitable Lions to the Olympic title in Sydney in 2000 and the Africa Cup of Nations in 2000 and 2002.

PROFESSIONAL

A canny businessman, Eto'o founded his own phone company, Eto'o Télécom, in 2011.

MAJOR HONOURS

Olympic gold medal (2000)

African Cup of Nations (2000, 2002)

Spanish Cup (2003, 2009)

Champions League (2006, 2009, 2010)

Serie A (2010)

Club World Cup 2010

Italian Cup (2010, 2011)

La Liga (2005, 2006, 2009)

LUCKY CHARM

In extraordinary back-to-back seasons, Samuel Eto'o won two successive treble titles (championship, national cup, and Champions League) with two different clubs: in 2009 with Barcelona and in 2010 with Inter Milan.

EVERYBODY IN THEIR PLACE

Samuel Eto'o is famed for his high opinion of himself and for his oversized ego. He boldly proclaimed: "I didn't play with Lionel Messi; Lionel Messi played with me."

24

SELF-ASSURED

Eto'o appears so self-confident that he can seem arrogant.

CAMEROONIAN
117 international games
56 international goals

DATES
Born in 1981

POSITION
Centre forward

MAIN CLUBS
Barcelona, Inter Milan

SCORING MACHINE

He is the top-scorer in the history of the Cameroon national team and the Africa Cup of Nations!

MISSILE LAUNCHER

Eto'o is one of very few naturally two-footed players, who was just as accurate and powerful with his favoured right as his left.

The indomitable lion

Zlatan Ibrahimovic

INCREDIBLE

A global superstar, five different stamps celebrating the Swedish attacker have been issued since 2014.

This maverick Swede with the giant ego, born of a Bosnian father and Croatian mother, has traveled the globe playing for the world's greatest clubs: the Netherlands with Ajax; Italy with Inter Milan then AC Milan; Spain with Barcelona; France with PSG and the UK with Manchester United; he has scored over 350 goals, including countless stunners. Brash and outspoken off the pitch, but deadly on the pitch, in 2017 he became the second-most decorated active football player in the world, with 32 trophies to his name.

MAJOR HONOURS

Serie A (2007, 2008, 2009, 2011)

UEFA Super Cup (2009)

Club World Cup (2009)

La Liga (2010)

French Championship (2013, 2014, 2015, 2016)

English League Cup (2017)

MOUTHY

Ibrahimovic isn't known for his modesty. When he left PSG, he said: "I came like a king, left like a legend." But it's true that he was voted the French championship's best player three times in four years between 2013 and 2016!

AMAZING GOAL

Ibrahimovic scored his most spectacular goal in 2012, in an international match against England. The goalkeeper, who was a long way outside his area, headed the ball clear and Zlatan scored with a 30-metre bicycle kick. It was his fourth goal of the match!

FAIR PLAY

A volcanic presence, he was yellow carded more than 100 times during his career.

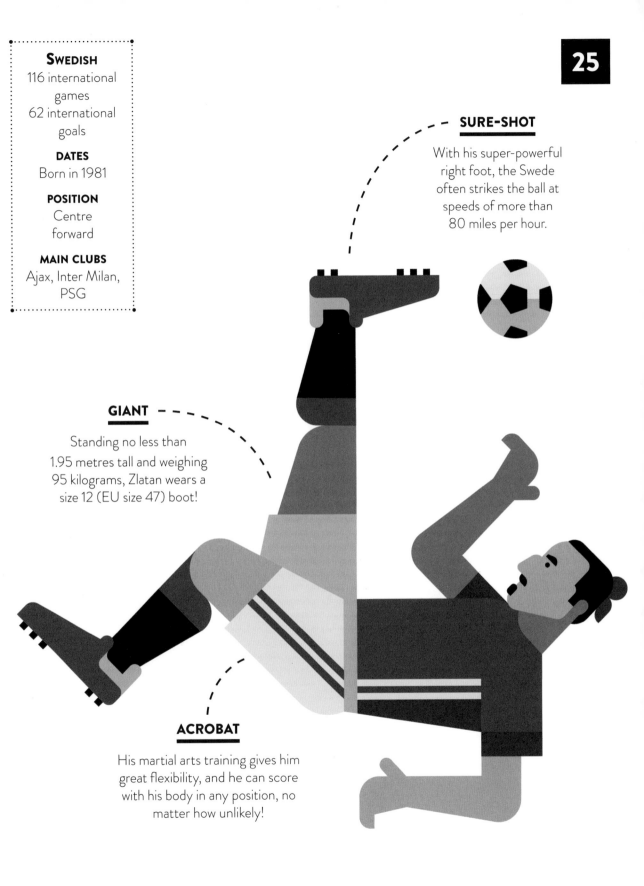

25

SWEDISH
116 international games
62 international goals

DATES
Born in 1981

POSITION
Centre forward

MAIN CLUBS
Ajax, Inter Milan, PSG

SURE-SHOT

With his super-powerful right foot, the Swede often strikes the ball at speeds of more than 80 miles per hour.

GIANT

Standing no less than 1.95 metres tall and weighing 95 kilograms, Zlatan wears a size 12 (EU size 47) boot!

ACROBAT

His martial arts training gives him great flexibility, and he can score with his body in any position, no matter how unlikely!

Ibracadabra

Megan Rapinoe

A gold medallist at the London Olympics in 2012 and a two-time World Cup winner (2015 and 2019), Megan Rapinoe is, along with Alex Morgan, the undeniable star of the US team and of women's football. Although she plays in midfield, she scores more goals than many strikers. Unusually for a footballer, this multi-talented player also has a degree in sociology and political science. She is just as famous for her personality and her activism as she is for her skills on the pitch.

TRANSFER

At 27, Megan Rapinoe spent six months playing for French club Olympique Lyonnais and won three titles!

> " Yes, we play sports. Yes, we play soccer. Yes, we are female athletes, but we are so much more than that.,,

AWARDS

Megan Rapinoe won the women's Ballon d'Or in 2019.

FIGHTER

An advocate for LGBT rights and a campaigner against police brutality towards African Americans, Megan Rapinoe also took a stand against Donald Trump's policies.

RESPECT US!

Megan Rapinoe is her teammates' spokesperson in the fight for equal pay. The US women's team have dominated their sport for years but are paid less than the men's team.

MAJOR HONOURS

Olympic gold medal (2012)

Championne de French National League (2013, 2014)

French Cup (2013)

World Cup (2015, 2019)

26

STYLISH

She likes to change her look and dyes her hair pink or purple.

CELEBRATION

After scoring, she does her signature celebration, spreading her arms wide.

AMERICAN
158 international games
50 international goals

DATES
Born 5th July 1985

POSITION
Left winger

MAIN CLUBS
Chicago Red Stars, Olympique Lyonnais, Reign FC

MISSION ACCOMPLISHED

At the 2019 World Cup, she scored six times and won the Golden Boot and Ballon d'Or awards.

The icon

Ronaldo

The greatest modern centre forward, Ronaldo Luis Nazário de Lima, known as Ronaldo, struck fear into defenses as a player for Brazil as well as for his club sides in his homeland, the Netherlands, Italy, and Spain. He was already successful as a teenager, heading to Europe at the age of 17 when he signed for PSV Eindhoven, and made an instant impression with 36 goals in 35 matches during his first season. A powerful and explosive attacker, he possessed fabulous technique for a man of his size, combined with extraordinary ball control.

A WINNING START

During his second international match for Brazil, against Iceland, he scored, set another one up and won a penalty. This was just the beginning. By the end of his career, Ronaldo had scored an average of 0.63 goals per international match.

MAJOR HONOURS

World Cup
(1994, 2002)

Copa America
(1997, 1999)

Cup Winners' Cup
(1997)

UEFA Cup
(1998)

La Liga
(2003, 2007)

Brazilian Cup
(1993, 2009)

Intercontinental
Cup (2002)

THE SPECIALIST

Ronaldo played at four World Cups: he won two winner's medals, was once a beaten finalist and once eliminated in the quarter-finals. In 2002, he was the competition's top scorer, with eight goals, and was voted man of the match in the final!

TRANSFERS

He played for seven different clubs between 1993 and 2011.

15
World Cup
goals

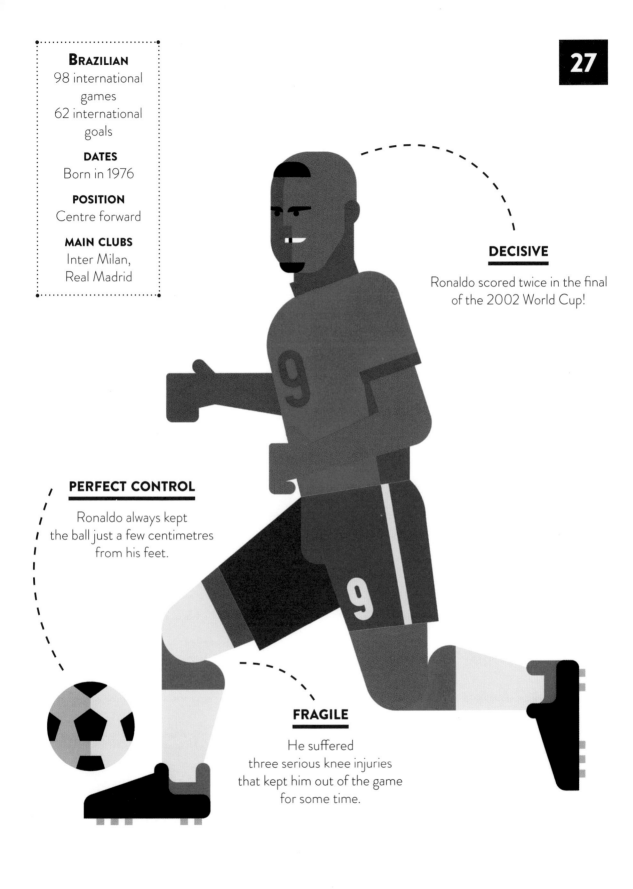

27

BRAZILIAN
98 international games
62 international goals

DATES
Born in 1976

POSITION
Centre forward

MAIN CLUBS
Inter Milan, Real Madrid

DECISIVE
Ronaldo scored twice in the final of the 2002 World Cup!

PERFECT CONTROL
Ronaldo always kept the ball just a few centimetres from his feet.

FRAGILE
He suffered three serious knee injuries that kept him out of the game for some time.

Il fenomeno

Andrés Iniesta

The Barcelona star, who has spent his entire career at one club, is a fantastically accomplished midfielder. He boasts one of the finest collections of winner's medals in soccer history, for both club and country. Barcelona's number 8 was at times overshadowed by stars like Ronaldinho, Eto'o, and Messi, but everything at the Nou Camp went through the little Spanish magician. He is the only player ever to be named Man of the Match in the final of the World Cup, the European Championship, and the Champions League!

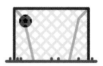

LEGENDARY GOAL

He secured Spain's first-ever World Cup in 2010 with the only goal of the final against Holland. His strike came in extra-time, with just four minutes remaining.

33
trophies won

MAJOR HONOURS

Champions League (2006, 2009, 2011, 2015)

La Liga (2005, 2006, 2009, 2010, 2011, 2013, 2015)

European Championship (2008, 2012)

UEFA Super Cup (2009, 2011, 2015)

World Cup (2010)

Club World Cup (2011, 2015)

ADMIRED BY ALL

In November 2015, Barcelona humbled deadly rivals Real Madrid, by beating them 4-0 at home. Even so, Andrés Iniesta left the field to the sound of applause from the crowd at the Santiago Bernabeu ground.

PURE CLASS

"Lionel Messi is the greatest, but Iniesta is the one who plays the best football," according to the mighty Juan Riquelme, replaced by Iniesta in the Barcelona team.

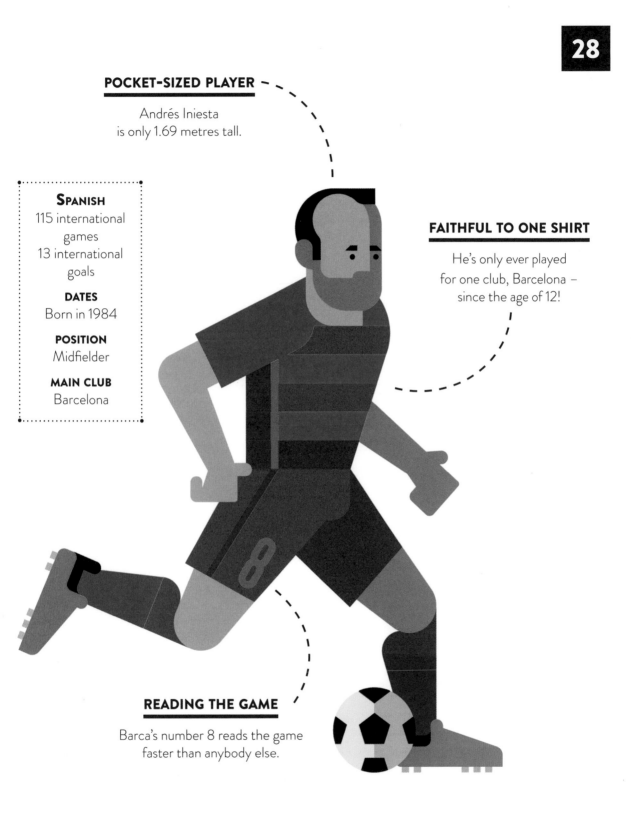

28

POCKET-SIZED PLAYER

Andrés Iniesta
is only 1.69 metres tall.

SPANISH
115 international
games
13 international
goals

DATES
Born in 1984

POSITION
Midfielder

MAIN CLUB
Barcelona

FAITHFUL TO ONE SHIRT

He's only ever played
for one club, Barcelona –
since the age of 12!

READING THE GAME

Barca's number 8 reads the game
faster than anybody else.

The maestro

Cristiano Ronaldo

287

goals in Spain's La Liga

A star at Manchester United, then Real Madrid, Cristiano Ronaldo has only one contemporary rival: Lionel Messi. Trained at Sporting Lisbon, he completely reinvented his playing style over just a few years. His succession of drag-backs, step-overs and nutmegs were refocused with a single goal in mind: the opponent's! Dubbed CR7 in honour of his prized number 7 shirt, he holds the record for the most goals scored in a single Champions League season (17). He is also the first player in La Liga to have scored over 30 goals in every season!

MAJOR HONOURS

Premier League (2007, 2008, 2009)

European Championship (2016)

Club World Cup (2008, 2014)

La Liga (2012)

Champions League (2008, 2014, 2016)

SERIAL STRIKER

Cristiano Ronaldo is one of the all-time great attackers: in Spain, nobody scored more goals than he did in the 2008, 2011, 2014 and 2015 seasons. This achievement is all the greater since Cristiano doesn't play as an out-and-out centre forward.

RECORD WINNER

In September 2015, he overtook the legendary Raul and his 228 goals for Real in the Spanish champinship, scoring 5 goals away against Espanyol. It took Raul 550 matches to set his record, but Ronaldo needed just 203 games to beat it.

AWARDS

Cristiano Ronaldo won the Ballon d'Or in 2008, 2013, 2014 and 2016.

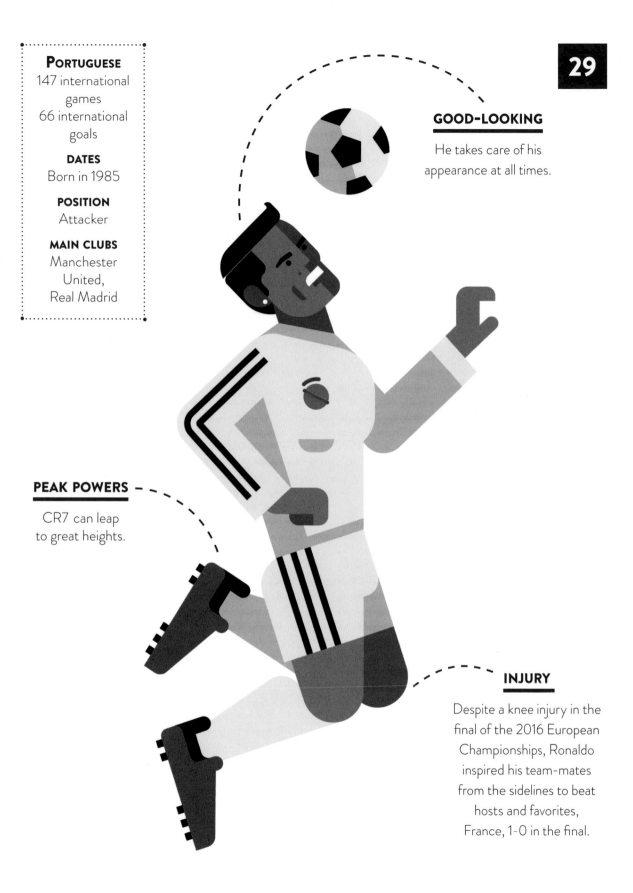

29

PORTUGUESE
147 international games
66 international goals

DATES
Born in 1985

POSITION
Attacker

MAIN CLUBS
Manchester United,
Real Madrid

GOOD-LOOKING
He takes care of his appearance at all times.

PEAK POWERS
CR7 can leap to great heights.

INJURY
Despite a knee injury in the final of the 2016 European Championships, Ronaldo inspired his team-mates from the sidelines to beat hosts and favorites, France, 1-0 in the final.

Heading for goal!

Mohamed Salah

After a bright start to his career in his native Egypt, Mohamed Salah played for Basel, Chelsea, Fiorentina, Roma and then Liverpool, which became his long-term club. The Premier League's top goal-scorer in the 2017/18 season, he is a multi-talented, fast, creative and incredibly effective attacker. Salah helped Egypt to reach the final of the African Cup of Nations, where they lost 2-1 to Cameroon, and to qualify for the World Cup after 28 years of waiting!

INCREDIBLE

In May 2018, the British Museum included his football boots in an exhibition of Egyptian artefacts.

AWARDS

In 2017 and 2018, he was voted African Player of the Year.

6

he has scored for every one of his six professional clubs.

POPULAR

Mohamed Salah is a true icon in his home country. He won 1 million votes at the last Egyptian presidential election, although he wasn't even a candidate!

DISAPPOINTMENT!

Thanks to Salah's footballing talent, Liverpool reached the Champions League final in 2018. They played Real Madrid, but Salah was injured at the start of the match and the Reds lost 3-1.

MAJOR HONOURS

Swiss Championship (2013, 2014)

Champions League (2019)

30

EGYPTIAN
67 international games,
41 international goals

DATES
Born 15th June 1992

POSITION
Attacker

MAIN CLUBS
AC Fiorentina,
AS Roma,
Liverpool FC

GOAL!

He has some iconic goal celebrations including making an 'x' with his arms and praying.

A RED THROUGH AND THROUGH

He is hugely popular among the home supporters at Anfield!

THREE MAGIC INGREDIENTS

Perfect first touches, amazing speed and brilliant ball control make him a master footballer.

The Pharaoh

Sergio Ramos

MAJOR HONOURS

World Cup (2010)

European Championship (2008, 2012)

La Liga (2007, 2008, 2012)

Spanish Cup (2011, 2014)

Champions League (2014, 2016)

UEFA Super Cup (2014, 2016, 2017)

Club World Cup (2014, 2016)

Trained at Seville, Sergio Ramos became a star at Real Madrid by playing in both the center of defence and at full-back. Iron-willed inside his own area, Sergio Ramos is also an unlikely goalscorer, chalking up over 20 goals in his first four seasons at Real. He also scored in two Champions League finals, an exceptional achievement for a defender. An international since 2005, Ramos is one of history's most-capped outfield players, with 130 international games at the last count.

HOBBY
He loves bull-fighting, and at one stage considered it as a career.

10
international goals

SKIN DEEP

After winning the World Cup in 2010 in South Africa, Sergio Ramos had a tattoo of the World Cup trophy inked into his forearm.

CHAMPION!

As part of the Spanish national team, Sergio Ramos is one of seven players to have won Euro 2008, the World Cup 2010 and Euro 2012 as first choice players in their position, a triple crown unprecedented in the history of world football.

SPANISH
147 international
games
11 international
goals

DATES
Born in 1986

POSITION
Central defender

MAIN CLUB
Real Madrid

AIR POWER –
Excellent at heading
the ball, he also scored many
goals, often match-winners.

2 X 2
At Real Madrid,
Sergio Ramos wears
the number 4, the same
number as the legendary
Fernando Hierro.

A BORN LEADER
Ramos captained
Real Madrid
and Spain.

The warrior

Lionel *Messi*

Born in Rosario, the Argentinian star has ruled football for the past decade and more. Capable of astonishing acceleration, Messi is a left-footer with an amazing dribble, able to beat several players in a very small area. His exceptional talents helped Barcelona to win twenty or so titles during the years 2005 to 2011, including four Champions Leagues. Known as *Pulga* (the flea), Messi had less luck with Argentina: his only title with the national team being the gold medal at the 2008 Olympics.

AWARDS
Messi has won the Ballon d'Or five times, an all-time record.

FAIR PLAY
Mild-mannered Lionel was sent off during his first international match.

MAJOR HONOURS

Club World Cup (2009, 2011, 2015)

Champions League (2006, 2009, 2011, 2015)

La Liga (2005, 2006, 2009, 2010, 2011, 2013, 2015, 2016)

Olympic Gold (2008)

Spanish Cup (2009, 2012, 2015, 2016, 2017)

UEFA Super Cup (2009, 2011, 2015)

Aged **28** had already won 28 titles

HIS LEGENDARY GOAL

On 18 April 2007, aged just 19, Messi was playing in a semi-final of the Spanish Cup against Getafe. Picking up the ball in his half, he advanced up the pitch, dribbling past six players before shooting into the empty net. A star was born!

FOOTBALL IN THE BLOOD

"What's great about Lionel is that he plays today just like he used to play when he was a 12-year-old," said Carles Rexach, the man who recruited Messi for Barcelona in 2000.

32

ARGENTINIAN
122 international games
61 international goals

DATES
Born in 1987

POSITION
Attacking midfielder

MAIN CLUB
Barcelona

MASSIVE PLAYER

Messi is just 1.69 metres tall but he still scores headers, including in the Champions League final in 2009, where Barcelona beat Manchester United 2-0.

10 OUT OF 10

Messi wears his favourite number for club and country.

SURE-SHOT

He is the top scorer in the history of La Liga, the Spanish league.

The little prince

N'Golo Kante

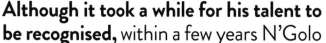

Although it took a while for his talent to be recognised, within a few years N'Golo Kanté quickly established himself as one of the best defensive players in the world. After playing for smaller clubs Caen and Leicester, the tireless midfielder signed for Chelsea and was picked for the French national team. Although he's only 1.69 metres tall, Kanté's quick feet and fighting spirit mean he pounces on any loose ball and always makes his team play better. His last two clubs have both won the Premier League, and the French national team won the 2018 World Cup, so he must be doing something right!

INCREDIBLE

In 2011 he was still playing amateur football, and seven years later he was a World Champion!

1

international goal

MULTI-TALENTED

Before signing his first professional contract at 22, the midfielder managed to earn an accounting qualification.

REJECTED

At first the midfielder was rejected by professional teams because they thought he was too small.

MAJOR HONOURS

Premier League (2016, 2017)

FA Cup (2018)

World Cup (2018)

33

CHARMER

He has left all of his previous teams
on very good terms and is well liked
by his teammates.

FRENCH
39 international
games,
1 international goal

DATES
Born 29th
March 1991

POSITION
Midfielder

MAIN CLUB
Chelsea

KING OF TACKLES

He is brilliant at tackling,
recovering and running
off with the ball.

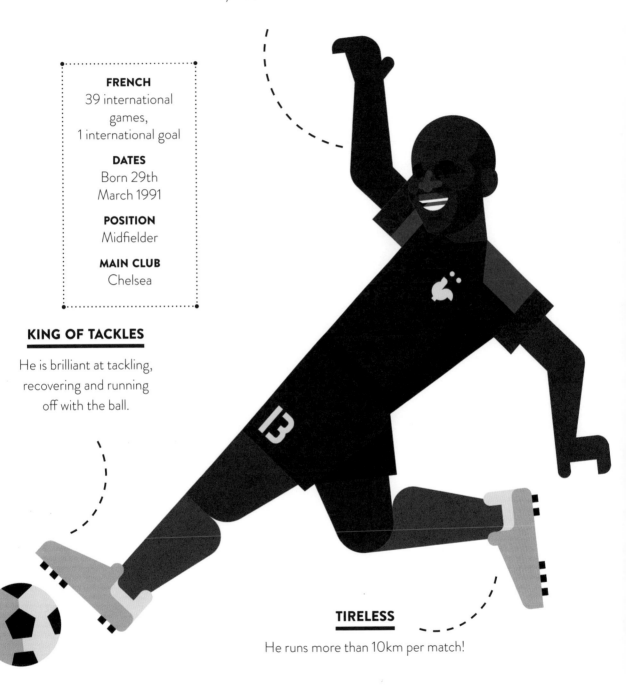

TIRELESS

He runs more than 10km per match!

Late bloomer

Paul Pogba

MAJOR HONOURS

Italian Cup (2015, 2016)

Serie A (2013, 2014, 2015, 2016)

English League Cup (2017)

Europa League (2017)

FAIR PLAY

In 2013, he was yellow-carded twice in three minutes during an international match against Spain!

Released as a promising teenager by Manchester United, Pogba moved to Juventus and quickly established himself as a first-choice pick for the club and the French national team. Nick-named pioche, meaning pickaxe, the lanky 1.91-metre tall Pogba is an expert at stealing the ball off opponents as well as beating them one-on-one. The model of today's player, he can be the playmaker, beat defenders with his amazing dribbles, or score from distance with his thunderous shot; qualities that encouraged United to stump up a then-world-record fee of £89million to re-sign him in the summer of 2016.

AWARD

Paul Pogba was voted Young Player of the Tournament at the 2014 World Cup.

4

times Champion of Italy aged just 23

LEGENDARY GOAL

During the 2015-2016 Serie A season, Pogba scored a sumptuous 25-metre volley, which stunned the opposing Napoli keeper. The Juventus midfielder's volleyed goal was as perfect as it was powerful.

FUTURE STAR

Rio Ferdinand, the legendary Manchester United defender and former captain of England, has no doubts about Paul Pogba's talent: "He's world-class. He's a potential winner of the Ballon d'Or."

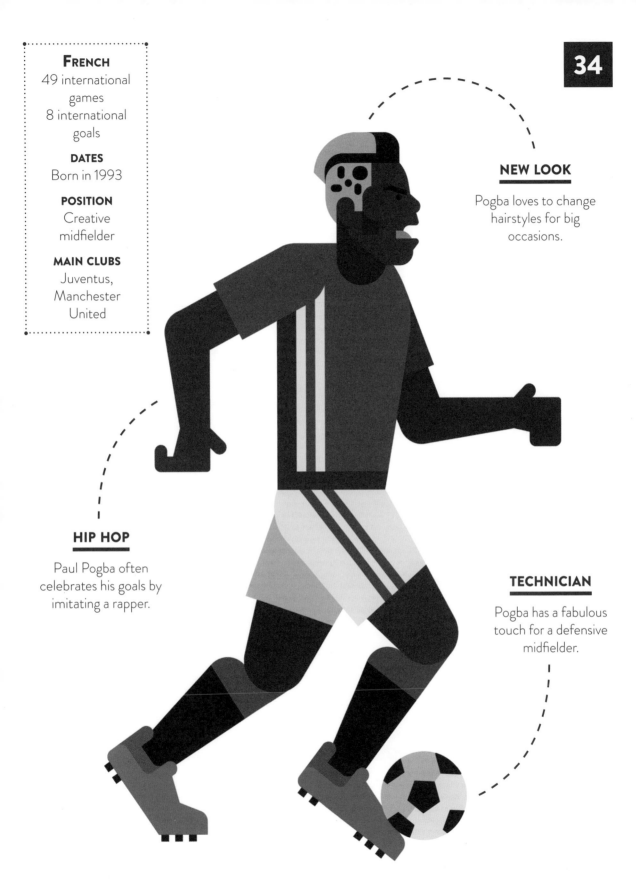

34

FRENCH
49 international games
8 international goals

DATES
Born in 1993

POSITION
Creative midfielder

MAIN CLUBS
Juventus, Manchester United

NEW LOOK
Pogba loves to change hairstyles for big occasions.

HIP HOP
Paul Pogba often celebrates his goals by imitating a rapper.

TECHNICIAN
Pogba has a fabulous touch for a defensive midfielder.

Head-turning style

Neymar

Like Pele before him, Neymar learned his trade at Brazilian club Santos and has since become the most expensive footballer on the planet. He made his name at Barcelona as a prolific goal-scorer, peerless technician and gifted dribbler. Playing alongside Messi at Barca, the two fought for the title of the world's greatest player, and in 2017, Neymar stepped out of Messi's shadow and moved to Paris-Saint Germain in the most controversial transfer in football history. The mega-rich club paid £200 million to bring him to France.

PROFESSIONAL
At the age of 25, Neymar owned a private jet, a helicopter and a yacht.

MAJOR HONOURS

Brazilian Cup (2010)

Confederations Cup (2013)

Copa Libertadores (2011)

La Liga (2015, 2016)

Spanish Cup (2015, 2016)

Club World Cup (2015)

Champions League (2015)

Olympic Gold (2016)

INCREDIBLE
There is already a statue of Neymar on display at Madame Tussaud's in London.

14
years old: first professional contract

WHAT A GOAL!
In 2011, Neymar was playing against Flamengo. Starting from the centre of the pitch, Santos' centre forward dribbled past two opponents, played a one-two with a teammate, then nutmegged the last defender before scoring. A masterpiece, voted the greatest goal of the year by FIFA!

ALMOST
In 2005, the Brazilian was approached by Real Madrid who wanted to look at him at the same time as Robinho. The young prodigy was only 13 at the time, but Madrid were convinced. Sadly for them, Santos refused the transfer.

35

A CUT ABOVE

Neymar's hairstyles are always closely watched.

BRAZILIAN
75 international games
50 international goals

DATES
Born in 1992

POSITION
Forward

MAIN CLUBS
Barcelona, PSG

A VIRTUOSO

Drag-back, double touches, high-speed step-overs, Neymar is a born dribbler.

AN EARLY STARTER

He captained Brazil aged just 23.

Ultra-creative

Kylian Mbappé

TRANSFERS

At 18, he was signed by Paris Saint-Germain for 180 million euros!

Talent-spotted at a very young age, Kylian Mbappé moves fast both on the pitch and in his career. He was signed by Monaco in 2013 and quickly became one of the brightest stars of the French Championship, setting records as the club's youngest ever goal-scorer and the youngest player in history to score in the semi-finals of the Champions League. Many of the biggest clubs in the world wanted to sign him, and he joined the superstar Neymar at Paris Saint-Germain. The whole world discovered his talent at the 2018 World Cup, where he scored four goals for France, including one in the final!

MAJOR HONOURS

French Championship (2017, 2018, 2019)

French Cup (2018)

World Cup (2018)

INCREDIBLE

In 2019, he became the youngest player in history to score 50 goals in the French Championship.

PRECOCIOUS

At 19, the French attacker became the youngest player to score in a World Cup final since Pelé in 1958.

KNIGHTED

"If Kylian keeps on equalling my records like this, I may have to dust my boots off again." This badge of honour came from the legendary Pelé.

10

goals for France, before he'd even turned 20!

36

STAR POSITION

He plays in number 10, a number also worn by megastars, Platini and Zidane.

FRENCH
34 international games,
13 international goals

DATES
Born 20th December 1998

POSITION
Attacker

MAIN CLUBS
Monaco, Paris Saint-Germain

CELEBRATION

When he scores a goal, he calmly crosses his arms and soaks in the glory.

SERIOUS SPEED

His most amazing tactic is to outrun everyone around him.

The teen wonder

Mia Hamm

The most famous women's footballer of the 1990s, the American attacker played most of her career for her university team before the creation of a US professional soccer league. She became famous around the world as a player with the US national side, dazzling with her brilliant technique, powerful shot and excellent finishing. Voted Best American Player each year from 1994 to 1998, she remains an extremely popular figure, even after her retirement from the game.

INCREDIBLE

Soccer Barbie was named after her, and her kit sponsor, Nike, also has a building named in her honour.

PROFESSIONAL

She made her international debut in 1987, aged just 15!

275
selections

MULTI-TALENTED

Midfielder or attacker, Hamm even played goalkeeper once during a match against Denmark after the main goalie was sent off and so couldn't be replaced.

DOUBLE SUCCESS

She won her second World Cup in 1999, in a tournament hosted by the USA, with the home team winning the final against China on penalties. The match was watched by over 90,000 spectators, a US record for a women's sporting event.

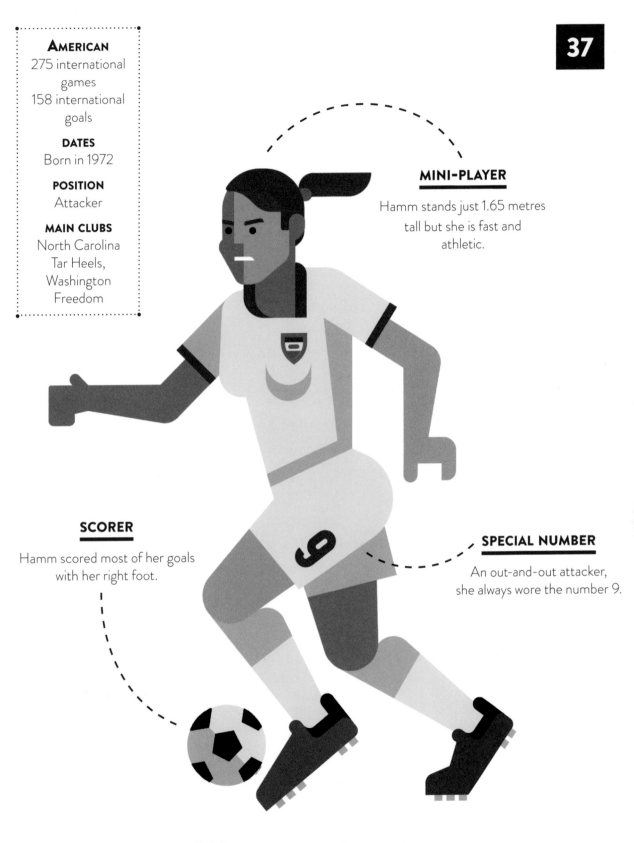

37

AMERICAN
275 international
games
158 international
goals

DATES
Born in 1972

POSITION
Attacker

MAIN CLUBS
North Carolina
Tar Heels,
Washington
Freedom

MINI-PLAYER

Hamm stands just 1.65 metres
tall but she is fast and
athletic.

SCORER

Hamm scored most of her goals
with her right foot.

SPECIAL NUMBER

An out-and-out attacker,
she always wore the number 9.

Woman with the golden feet

Ada Hegerberg

No one can stand in the way of incredible Norwegian attacker **Ada Hegerberg**, who has dominated women's football since 2016. A key player at French club Olympique Lyonnais, she has unbelievable speed, power and touch on the ball. Since joining Lyon, she has scored 187 goals in 149 matches, an exceptional record. In 2018, the Norwegian wrote herself into the Champions League history books by scoring 15 goals, one of which was when her team beat Wolfsburg in the final.

INCREDIBLE

She scored her 250th club goal when she was only 23 years old.

14

that's how old she was when she started her playing career in Norway.

MAJOR HONOURS

French Championship (2015, 2016, 2017, 2018, 2019)

French Cup (2015, 2016, 2017, 2019)

Champions League (2016, 2017, 2018, 2019)

Ballon d'Or (2018)

WINNER

In 2018, she won the first ever women's Ballon d'Or and said, "It's a huge step for women's football. Young girls around the world, believe in yourselves."

A FAMILY AFFAIR

Ada Hegerberg was born into a family of football fans. Her older sister Andrine is a midfielder at Italian team Roma.

38

NORWEGIAN
66 international
games

DATES
Born 10th July
1995

POSITION
Attacker

MAIN CLUB
Olympique
lyonnais

THE STAR IN THE CROWN

She signed a golden
contract with
Olympique Lyonnais.

14

She is proud to wear the
same number on her
shirt as her childhood
idol, Thierry Henry.

UNSTOPABLE

She scored 25 goals in
one season!

The pioneer

Marta

She was recruited at the age of **14** by the club Vasco de Gama

Small in stature but immense in talent, Marta is probably the greatest-ever women's footballer. Taught to play by her brothers in the streets of Dois Riachos in north-eastern Brazil, she learnt to play in a style that was instinctive, fast and incredibly creative. Scouted at an early age, she was an international player at the World Cup at the age of just 17 – the same age as Brazil's idol, Pelé. A highly talented live-wire, Marta is the undisputed star of women's football in Brazil. But she hasn't yet fulfilled her dream of winning the World Cup!

MAJOR HONOURS

Pan American Games gold medal (2003, 2007)

Champions League (2004)

Swedish Championship (2005, 2006, 2007, 2008, 2012)

TRANSFER

Marta has played for ten clubs in Brazil, the USA and Sweden.

A LEGEND

FIFA named her Women's Player of the Year five times in succession, from 2006 to 2010. No other woman can match this achievement, made all the more impressive by the fact that she also came second in this prestigious line-up no less than four times.

PIONEER

A cast of her foot was immortalised in concrete at the Maracanã stadium in Rio de Janeiro after her winning appearance in the final of the 2007 Pan American Games. She is the first woman to join the giants of Brazilian football being honoured in this way.

39

STRIKE RATE !

Marta scored almost a goal a game in international games.

BRAZILIAN
95 international games
92 international goals

DATES
Born in 1986

POSITION
Attacker

MAIN CLUBS
Santos FC,
FC Rosengård

AIR POWER

Marta scores from any position.

THE STAR

She wears the same number as Pelé.

The Brazilian pear

Amandine Henry

Capped by France over 50 times, an unbreakable shield in front of the defence, Amandine Henry is the queen of the midfield, where she is known for her ability to retrieve the ball from the opposing team and for the exceptional accuracy of her passing. Very technically gifted, powerful and an outstanding striker of the ball, the French international was the second highest scorer at the 2015 World Cup in Canada. Her defensive and attacking prowess is recognised all over the world.

9

French championship titles

AWARD

Amandine Henry won the Ballon d'Argent at the 2015 World Cup.

MAJOR HONOURS

French Championship (2008, 2009, 2010, 2011, 2012, 2013, 2014, 2015, 2016)

French Cup (2012, 2013, 2014, 2015, 2016)

Champions League (2011, 2012, 2016)

SUCCESS IN THE USA

Amandine Henry signed to the Portland Thorns in 2016. She is the fifth French woman to play for a pro team in US soccer, but the first who was already a star upon signing.

SUPERSONIC SHOT

During a France-Mexico match at the 2015 World Cup, Amandine Henry shot from a distance of almost 30 metres. The ball flew high into the back of the Mexican net, with the goalie unable to stop such a fierce and powerful strike.

40

FRENCH
63 international
games
7 international
goals

DATES
Born in 1989

POSITION
Midfielder

MAIN CLUB
Olympique
Lyonnais

ALL-ROUNDER

Amandine Henry is
right-footed but she also scores
fabulous goals with her left.

A NOBLE NUMBER

Whether playing for France
or with her clubs, Amandine Henry
always wears the number 6 shirt.

OUCH!

Troubled for a long time
by a painful knee, she had a
surgical cartilage graft!

The conqueror

Timeline

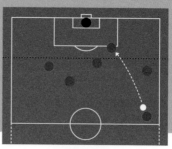

1863

The creation, in England, of the very first football association and adoption of the first 17 laws of the game.

Football and rugby officially seperate.

1925

The offside law changes: the minimum number of players between the attacker and the goal is cut from three to two at the moment the ball is played to the attacker. Here, it's a definite offside.

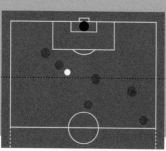

1866

The offside rule at the time was: at least three players must be between the attacker and the goal. Here, the blue player with the ball is offside.

1930

The first World Cup is staged in Uruguay, South America.

1930–1950

The English popularised the formation WM, with three defenders, two defensive midfielders, two attacking midfielders and three attackers. The attacking line forms a W, and the defenders form an M.

1891

The penalty arrives. Before 1902, penalties could be taken from anywhere along the line marked out 12 yards from the goal.

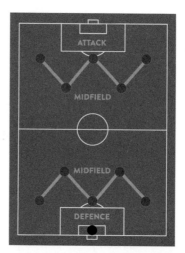

1963

A formation known as *catenaccio* dominates the game in Europe. Perfected at Inter Milan, it is a counter-attack system that uses eight players in defence to nulllify attacks.

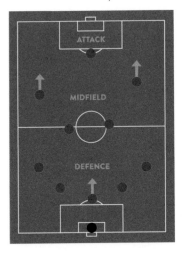

ATTACK

MIDFIELD

DEFENCE

1970s

Originating with Ajax Amsterdam, total football requires every single player to attack and defend!

1990

Players are required to wear shin pads during matches.

The Premier League is created in 1992. Today, it is the most-watched domestic football competition in the world.

1991

The first Women's World Cup is held in China.

1995

The offside rule changes again – only players who are considered to be actively involved in the move are now offside

SINCE 2015

Video Assistant Referee (VAR) was adopted for the 2018 World Cup and major competitions. A controversial technology, it has had a decisive role in the results of some games.

Inspiring | Educating | Creating | Entertaining

Brimming with creative inspiration, how-to projects, and useful information to enrich your everyday life, Quarto Knows is a favourite destination for those pursuing their interests and passions. Visit our site and dig deeper with our books into your area of interest: Quarto Creates, Quarto Cooks, Quarto Homes, Quarto Lives, Quarto Drives, Quarto Explores, Quarto Gifts, or Quarto Kids.

Fantastic Footballers © 2017 Gallimard Jeunesse, Paris
Translation © 2018 Quarto Publishing plc.

First Published in 2017 in French by Gallimard Jeunesse, France.
First Published in 2018 in English by Wide Eyed Editions, an imprint of
The Quarto Group
The Old Brewery, 6 Blundell Street, London N7 9BH, United Kingdom.
T (0)20 7700 6700 F (0)20 7700 8066 **www.QuartoKnows.com**

A catalogue record for this book is available from the British Library.

ISBN 978-1-78603-146-4

The illustrations were created digitally
Set in Brandon Grotesque and Gotham Rounded

Manufactured in Guangdong, China CC012020

9

MIX
Paper from
responsible sources
FSC
www.fsc.org   FSC® C008047